GROS

SOUVENIR BOOKLET

to DANA
From.
INA.

BRIAN C. BURSEY

Printed and bound in Canada by Friesen Printers.

ISBN 1-55056-769-1

Front Cover: *Western Brook Pond, as viewed from the north rim. The cliffs surrounding this glacially carved lake are more than 600 metres high.*

Back Cover: *Bonne Bay, with Table Mountain and the community of Woody Point in the background.*

Right: *Gros Morne Mountain, elevation 806 metres.*

▶ Showy Lady's Slipper.

A young bull moose enjoys a meal of white birch. This non-indigenous species was first introduced to the Island of Newfoundland in 1878. There are now more than 8,000 moose in Gros Morne National Park, representing one of the highest population densities in the world.

◀ Lobster Cove Head Lighthouse, Rocky Harbour. Constructed in 1897, the lighthouse is now a museum.

Wreck of the S.S. Ethie. The passenger and freight steamer Ethie was wrecked on Martin's Point, south of Cow Head, on December 10, 1919. A pulley system between the ship and dry land allowed all the crew and passengers to be saved, including a baby who was brought ashore in a mailbag.

▶ Stag caribou in autumn, near St. Pauls.

Rock Ptarmigan, Gros Morne Mountain. These birds, slightly smaller than the more common willow ptarmigan, are found on high barren hilltops throughout western Newfoundland. Their colour ranges from snow white in winter to mottled grey/brown in summer, providing excellent camouflage.

The hiking trail to Western Brook Pond leads visitors past a series of small ponds and an abundance of wildflowers.

The Arches, a provincially maintained public beach, is located just outside the northern boundary of Gros Morne National Park. The site features a series of unusual wave-carved limestone formations.

Playful humpback whales may be found throughout Newfoundland and Labrador waters during the summer months. Adults can reach 15 metres in length and weigh 50 tonnes.

◀ A caribou swims across Western Brook Pond.

▶ Falls on Bakers Brook.

Fishing boats and lobster pots at Woody Point, Bonne Bay.

◀ The Pitcher Plant, floral emblem of Newfoundland and Labrador.

Sandy beaches line the Gulf of St. Lawrence at Shallow Bay, Cow Head.

Above and right: Six hundred metre cliffs line glacially carved Western Brook Pond. Although at one time a true fiord, changes in sea level following the last glacial period have left this 13 kilometre lake well inland from the Gulf of St. Lawrence.

Contradicting its name, the red fox occurs in a variety of colours, including yellow, brown, black and silver.

◀ Waterfall, Western Brook Pond.

Trout River

Fishing vessels at Rocky Harbour.

▶ Arethusa or Dragon's Mouth Orchids. These flowers were photographed on the trail leading to Western Brook Pond.

Snowshoe hares are found throughout Gros Morne National Park.

The Tablelands and Norris Point.

◀ The Tablelands loom behind Bonne Bay and the community of Woody Point.

◀ Gros Morne Mountain, as viewed from Woody Point.

Fishing gear lies piled on a wharf at Trout River.

Green Gardens. The hiking trail to Green Gardens rewards visitors with spectacular coastal scenery, including sea stacks and sea caves.

◀ Sea stack, Green Gardens.

The Tablelands. This area owes its distinct colouration to peridotite, a rusty brown rock which is toxic to most forms of vegetation. This rock, formed deep underground, has been forced to the surface near Trout River through the collision of the vast continental plates which make up the earth's crust. This unusual exposure was a prime reason for the designation of the Gros Morne area as a World Heritage Site by UNESCO.